READING POWER

Transportation Through the Ages

Planes of the Past

Mark Beyer

The Rosen Publishing Group's
PowerKids Press™
New York

Published in 2002 by The Rosen Publishing Group, Inc.
29 East 21st Street, New York, NY 10010

First Edition

Book Design: Christopher Logan

Photo Credits: Cover © Museum of Flight/Corbis; pp. 4–5, 9, 16–17 © Bettmann/Corbis; p. 7 © Museum of Flight/Corbis; p. 8 © Superstock; p. 11 © Hulton–Deutsch/Corbis; pp. 12–13 © Lake Country Museum/Corbis; pp. 14–15 © AP Wide World Photo; pp. 18–19, 20–21 © George Hall/Corbis

Beyer, Mark.
Planes of the past / Mark Beyer.
   p. cm. — (Transportation through the ages)
Includes bibliographical references and index.
ISBN 0-8239-5984-8 (library binding)
1. Airplanes—History—Juvenile literature. [1. Airplanes—History.]
I. Title.
TL670.3 .B48 2001
629.133'34'09—dc21
                                        2001000280

Manufactured in the United States of America

Contents

The First Planes

The first plane was built in 1903 by the Wright Brothers.

The plane flew 120 feet. It stayed in the air for 12 seconds. It did not have wheels to land on.

The Wright Brothers

Soon planes were built with bigger engines. Planes could fly faster and farther with the bigger engines. Wheels were added to planes to help them land safely.

Engine

Wheel

In 1927, Charles Lindbergh was the first pilot to make a solo nonstop flight across the Atlantic Ocean.

Lindbergh's plane was called
The Spirit of St. Louis.

Building Planes

Flying became popular in the 1930s. Planes were made in factories. Many planes could be built at the same time in a factory.

In the 1940s, larger planes were built to carry more people.

This plane could hold over 40 people. It flew 207 miles an hour.

Faster Planes

The first jet plane was flown in 1939. Jet planes could fly faster than other planes. They could also turn more easily in the air. This jet plane was flown in 1944.

Jet Engine

In 1947, Chuck Yeager was the first pilot to fly faster than the speed of sound. The speed of sound is 760 miles an hour.

Chuck Yeager

In the 1950s, passenger planes were built with jet engines. They could fly more than 500 miles an hour.

Top Speeds!

Airplane Type: 747
Speed: 640 mph

Airplane Type: 777
Speed: 615 mph

Airplane Type: 707
Speed: 600 mph

The first supersonic passenger jet
was built in the 1970s.

The supersonic jet can fly more than 1,000 miles an hour. Its success has changed the way people travel.

Glossary

factory (**fak**-tuhr-ee) a building where people make things

jet engine (**jeht ehn**-juhn) a plane engine that forcefully shoots out a jet of exhaust gases from the rear of the engine, driving the plane forward

nonstop (**nahn-stahp**) without stopping

popular (**pahp**-yuh-luhr) liked by most people

solo (**soh**-loh) without a partner; alone

supersonic (**soo**-puhr-sahn-ihk) able to move faster than the speed of sound

Resources

Books

100 Historic Airplanes in Full Color
by John H. Batchelor
Dover Publications (2000)

Research Planes
by David Baker
Rourke Enterprises (1987)

Web Site

"To Fly is Everything..."
http://hawaii.psychology.msstate.edu/
    invent/air_main.shtml

Index

Word Count: 238

Note to Librarians, Teachers, and Parents

If reading is a challenge, Reading Power is a solution! Reading Power is perfect for readers who want high-interest subject matter at an accessible reading level. These fact-filled, photo-illustrated books are designed for readers who want straightforward vocabulary, engaging topics, and a manageable reading experience. With clear picture/text correspondence, leveled Reading Power books put the reader in charge. Now readers have the power to get the information they want and the skills they need in a user-friendly format.